Dreamland

COLORING WHIMSICAL WORLDS

Renata Krawczyk

 **Get Creative 6**

NEW YORK

This book is dedicated to my
friends, who always support me.

Get Creative 6
An imprint of Mixed Media Resources
19 West 21st Street, Suite 601, New York, NY 10010
sixthandspringbooks.com

ISBN: 978-1-68462-034-0

Manufactured in China

3 5 7 9 10 8 6 4

First Edition

Introduction

I often find myself escaping from reality to the fairy-tale lands of my imagination. Magical places where unicorns, Thumbelina-size girls, and tiny deer frolic among teacups, paper boats, tree houses, and toadstools. I feel such peace when I allow my mind to wander in these lands and bring them to life in my drawings. I created this collection of coloring designs to invite you to visit this intimate world of my imagination and become a part of it.

All of the illustrations in this book were drawn by hand in pen and ink. I am very passionate about detail and this, hopefully, can be seen in most of my illustrations. When I draw, I start with a tiny dot and build the scenes piece by piece, filling them in with tiny elements. Smaller and larger circles are frequent elements in my drawings and create organic motifs. They provide interesting possibilities for interpretation and coloring.

Alongside fairy-tale themes, plant motifs prevail in the collection. My first degree was in biology, and I have always felt drawn to the natural world. I love surrounding myself with plants, and they often inspire my work. They offer a feeling of belonging, comfort, and well-being and stimulate my creative spirit. In my illustrations, I like to combine the plant world with fairy-tale elements, such as balloons, pennants, and paper boats.

My work often goes back to my childhood memories—forest wandering, braiding wreaths, and arranging bouquets of wildflowers. Small, mysterious country houses are another theme that have lately become an inspiration for my work. They are planted on trees, sprout from clover leaves, or fly away tied to balloons. The smallest of these houses are for birds.

Creating this collection of images has been such a joy. I am so excited to share these fantasy worlds with you as you color them and add your own dreams and imagination to them. I hope this book will serve as a "safe place" where time stands still.

—Renata

About the Author

Artist **Renata Krawczyk** was born in a small village in Poland and lives in the city of Lodz. After graduating with a degree in biology, she got a degree in fine arts and worked as a graphic designer. She now devotes her time entirely to illustration. Renata creates illustrations on the border between magical realism and fairy tales.

When she draws she starts with a tiny dot and builds the drawing piece by piece, filling it with tiny elements. She loves using textures and reinventing textures. She mostly draws with ink, but recently also started using mixed-media techniques with crayons, gouache, ink, and markers.

www.renaillustration.com

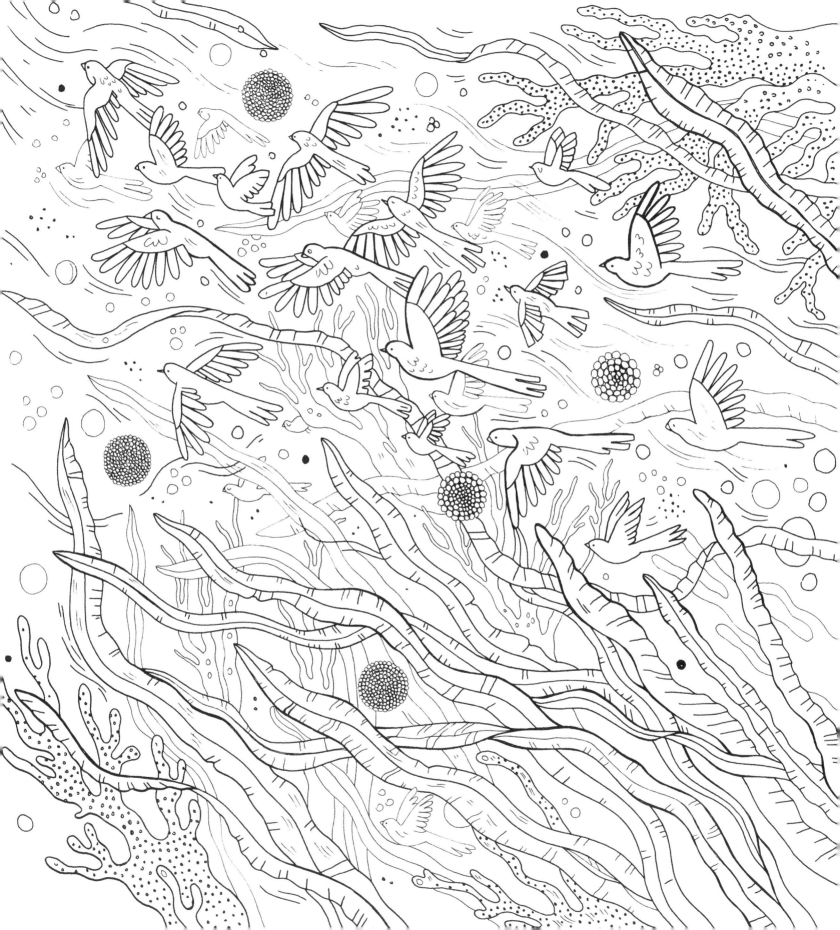

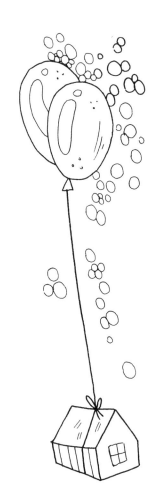